SCHOLASTIC
Time-to-Discover
READERS

D0472976

Arctic Animals

Melvin and Gilda Berger

SCHOLASTIC INC.
New York Toronto London Auckland Sydney
Mexico City New Delhi Hong Kong Buenos Aires

Photographs: Cover: Hartmut Schwarzbach/argus/Peter Arnold, Inc.;
p. 1: Tom Brakefield/Bruce Coleman Inc.; p. 3: Bryan & Cherry Alexander/arcticphoto.co.uk;
p. 4: Mitsuaki Iwago/Minden Pictures; p. 5: Bryan & Cherry Alexander/arcticphoto.co.uk;
p. 6: Mark Newman/Photo Researchers, Inc.; p. 7: Irwin & Peggy Bauer/Bruce Coleman Inc.;
p. 8: Bryan & Cherry Alexander/arcticphoto.co.uk; p. 9: Tom Brakefield/Bruce Coleman Inc.;
p. 10: Bryan & Cherry Alexander/arcticphoto.co.uk; p. 11: Flip Nicklin/Minden Pictures;
p. 12: Bryan & Cherry Alexander/arcticphoto.co.uk; p. 13: Francois Gohier/Photo Researchers Inc.;
p. 14: Bryan & Cherry Alexander/arcticphoto.co.uk; p. 15: Bryan & Cherry Alexander/arcticphoto.co.uk;
p. 16: Jean Francois Hellio & Nicholas Van Ingen/Photo Researchers, Inc.

Photo Research: Sarah Longacre

No part of this publication may be reproduced, or stored in a retrieval system,
or transmitted in any form or by any means, electronic, mechanical, photocopying,
recording, or otherwise, without written permission of the publisher. For information
regarding permission, write to Scholastic Inc., Attention: Permissions Department,
557 Broadway, New York, NY 10012.

ISBN 0-439-67901-X

Text copyright © 2005 by Melvin and Gilda Berger
All rights reserved. Published by Scholastic Inc.
SCHOLASTIC, SCHOLASTIC TIME-TO-DISCOVER READERS, and associated logos are
trademarks and/or registered trademarks of Scholastic Inc.

12 11 10 9 8 7 6 5 4 3 2 1   5 6 7 8 9 10/0

Printed in the U.S.A.
First Scholastic printing, January 2005

Arctic animals live around the North Pole.

Fun Fact

The Arctic is one of the coldest places on Earth.

The Arctic is very cold.

Snow and ice cover the Arctic.

Fun Fact
The Arctic is really an ocean of water covered by a thick layer of ice.

Polar bears live in the Arctic.

They walk on the ice.

Arctic foxes live in the Arctic.

Fun Fact

Arctic foxes often follow polar bears and eat their leftovers.

They hunt arctic hares.

Whales live in the Arctic.

They swim in big groups.

Seals live in the Arctic.

They come up for air.

Reindeer live in the Arctic.

They go far to find food.

Arctic animals are amazing!